The Smartest Man in the World
The Interview They Didn't Want You to See

The Smartest Man in the World

The Interview They Didn't Want You to See

Mega Foundation Press

Copyright © 2024
by Mega Foundation Press

All rights reserved. No part of this publication may be reproduced, stored or transmitted in any form or by any means, electronic, mechanical, photocopying, recording, scanning, or otherwise without written permission from the publisher. It is illegal to copy this book, post it to a website, or distribute it by any other means without permission. Mega Foundation Press is a trademark of the Mega Foundation, Inc.

ctmu.org
christopherlangan.com

First Paperback Edition

Published by
Mega Foundation Press
Princeton, MO

info@megapress.org

Typeset in Sabon
by Michał Szczęsny

Langan, C. M.

The Smartest Man in the World:
The Interview They Didn't Want You to See

1. Metaphysics 2. General Knowledge

ISBN 978-1-957661-00-1

Contents

Preface vii

The Interview 1

References 81

PREFACE

The Daily Wire is a conservative media company with HQ in Nashville, TN. It was founded in 2015 by Ben Shapiro and film director Jeremy Boreing. It's a leading online publisher with a notable presence on Facebook, and it produces video podcasts for people like Ben Shapiro, Jordan Peterson, and Candace Owens. It also repackages journalism from various news websites, usually with a conservative slant, and has released several feature-length films and two television series.

As the company has conservative leanings, there have been complaints that some of its content is unverified and that facts are twisted to fit its partisan perspective. But this is to be expected, as progressivists and their partisans always claim, usually on no evidence whatsoever, to have an exclusive lock on truth and reason. In fact, DW appears to be a respectable company.

I was interviewed by the DW on April 30 [2022] in Nashville. It must have cost the company several thousand dollars (including airfare, car fees, and overnight accommodations for my wife and me). They pressed me repeatedly to be interviewed on short notice by Michael Knowles, who conducted the interview in what seemed a very professional way. The idea was that Michael wanted to use the interview as the inaugural presentation in a special series he planned to introduce.

In the course of the interview, Gina and I met Michael, Jeremy (co-owner of the DW), and other members of the DW staff. Everyone claimed to love the interview, and not just a little. We expected to see it online within a couple of weeks.

But then it was pulled without explanation of any kind.

(...)

Excerpted from an article "High Strangeness at the Daily Wire" published on Chris Langan's Ultimate Reality *Substack.*

THE INTERVIEW

MK: Welcome to my extremely ethereal and trippy new set. I feel as though I am floating in a cloud here, in this all-white venue, and perhaps that is fitting for this first interview in a series of much longer, much more in-depth interviews. I'm so excited that my first guest is Christopher Langan, the smartest man in the world. I do not say that as a subjective statement or to flatter Chris. I mean that in as technical a way as possible. Chris has one of, if not the highest IQ ever recorded, somewhere between 190-195 and 210. And Chris is not here by way of some fancy, distinguished professorship at such and such brand name university, nor did Chris just get off of his private yacht, out of the south of France, and come here to leave his billion-dollar company. Chris came here from a farm in Missouri after a career as a bouncer at bars around New York.

Chris, thank you very much for coming on.

CML: Thank you for inviting me, Michael.

MK: I first stumbled onto you when I was eighteen years

old, a freshman in college, and—listen, I barely got out of high school math. I barely got out of calculus.

CML: I barely got out of high school myself.

MK: That's a good point. But I said, "This guy, he's saying things that are really, really interesting, and so I want to learn more." I've wanted to talk to you ever since then. I know that before we get into metaphysics, the existence of God, free will, politics, culture, and everything in between, I know people are going to be asking, "Why is the smartest man in the world not just buying and selling all of us all the time? Why is he living on a farm in the middle of Missouri?"

CML: Well, that's a good question. And it's that I was never actually interested in money. When I was a kid, my brothers and I, my family, we were not exactly the richest folks in town. We seldom had enough money to buy food or clothes, and so I immersed myself in books and reading and decided that what I wanted to do was pursue knowledge. It costs you nothing to pursue knowledge, really, provided you can sustain yourself while you're in pursuit of it. So that's what I did. I simply focused myself on, *I want to know the truth about reality. I want to know what kind of world it is that I'm living in.* And that's what I went for. Now, as far as the making of money is concerned, one thing that I found out is that there are certain ingredients, certain advantages, that you need in order to become rich. Of course, it helps to be born with money—

MK: (*laughs*) That's the easiest way.

CML: —and it helps to have a lot of connections, the

right kind of connections, and not to alienate the people who have all the money, because then they'll exclude you and cancel you. That's what they do. That's what cancel culture is. Basically, people are being frozen out of the economy. And I found myself getting frozen out of the economy that way from an early age. I tried to go to college but ran into a couple of problems, personnel problems, on the faculties of the colleges in question, and that stopped me. Basically, when you can't get a college education, you are canceled economically.

MK: Presumably though you show up to college. Even though you've got a tough upbringing and not any real advantages in terms of family or society you've got a higher IQ than anybody in the room. You're obviously extremely smart, extremely self-educated, so you get into college. It should be a total breeze for you.

CML: Well, it was a total breeze for me, too much of a breeze for me. You ask the wrong kinds of questions of people who are full of themselves and think they have all the answers. Like in a calculus class, "Why don't you explain what an infinitesimal interval is and how you can traverse from one end to the other?" and they'll look at you as though you've got two heads.

MK: I ask that all the time. I ask my waiters.

CML: *(laughs)* Well, I got a very poor reaction out of that. There was a math instructor, Albert Leisenring, I think, who decided that I must be absolutely brain-dead. This guy was a very strange character. He was about six and a half feet tall. He'd come into class. Everybody would be waiting there for him. He'd make a late entrance. We'd be waiting for 10-15 minutes. He'd walk in with this great big stack and mimeograph sheets, and then he'd hand them out—walk around the room, methodically handing out these sheets to all of the students, and everybody would've a sheet in front of him. Then he'd walk up to the room, and symbol for symbol, everything that was written on the sheets would appear on the blackboard. Then he'd turn around and walk out. I was having a hard time with this. There were certain things that I didn't quite understand—why he was doing them the way he was. So I kept on trying to track him down to his office. He was never in his office. I would wait in the hall for hours and hours but this guy never showed up. Finally, I caught him in his office and I said:

"Hi, Professor Leisenring, can I come in?"

"Well, I'm really kind of busy right now."

"I just wanted to ask you one question. Why do you do this? Why are you taking a set-theoretical approach to calculus like this? They don't seem to be compatible. On the one hand, calculus deals with change, whereas sets are static things. Why are you taking this particular approach to it?"

And he looks at me—Asperger's victim, right?—and he looks down at his thing, "Well, some people just don't have the mental firepower to be mathematicians." What was I supposed to do? Hit the guy? I wanted to hit him.

MK: Right, right, but he says something that's sort of pathetic almost to say.

CML: It is pathetic, but it basically told me a lot about how he sees the world, how he sees other people. I don't want to take a course from a guy like that, and it offended me because I'd been a poor kid. I just came off a ranch. I'd been working all summer punching cows and there I was. I meet all these—there was bunch of hippies in there—

MK: Right.

CML: —basically New York hippies. Now, I wouldn't call them hippies. These are basically affluent kids from New York. The place where I went was basically—that was the clientele, that was a student body. And they all were constantly talking, asking questions—bright for the most part, but I felt like a fish out of water. It was a culture shock for me. What is this? I'm used to being around a bunch of hay seeds. Cowboys—punching cows, going to the bar at night or whatever, drinking beer, and that was nothing like that. These kids were sitting around smoking pot, doing drugs, psychedelics—

MK: Now, just to clarify, when he says that not everyone has the power to be a mathematician—was this an admission of his own failure to explain his process, or is he calling you stupid?

CML: He was claiming that I didn't have the intellectual firepower to be a mathematician, or at least that's the way I interpreted it. And because I was used to being slighted in that way—I kind of grew up in a rough and tumble—if people feel intellectually threatened by you, you get a lot of this kind of thing up. So I assumed that that's what was happening and I've never seen or heard anything after that that would lead me to believe anything different.

MK: So, you leave college, presumably you're much more intelligent than anyone that you're going to meet on the faculty or in the students. So you leave college—what is it about being a bar bouncer? What is it about that physical activity? Because presumably even without a college degree, you could have done some middling paper-pushing job and it probably wouldn't have been very lucrative or fulfilling for you but, presumably you could have done something like that instead of a tough physical, potentially dangerous job, like your being a bouncer.

CML: I could have, but there are certain problems—for example, when I was in New York, I got a job in a grommet factory. It was Stimpson grommets. You had Grumman Aircraft there that got military defense contracts, and I think they were working on F-16's at one point. And then there was Stimpson grommets, which produced aircraft rivets for airplanes. And I had this machine—the sound, the noise from this machine—wham! wham! wham!—no hearing protection, and no nothing was issued to anybody. I started losing my hearing and so forth, and I figured, *Well, I can't stand this anymore. I got to get out of here.* I was about to leave, but I had a girlfriend, and she said, "No, I want you to stay." So I figured, *Okay, let me see if I can get another kind of job.* So I went and took the civil service exam and was offered a job by the IRS. And that of course was a moral dilemma.

MK: That's a fate worse than hell. (*laughs*)

CML: Exactly! How awful do I want to be as a person, you know? (*laughs*) And I decided that I needed to go home anyway, so I went back to Montana at that point. But basically then what I found out—I went back to New York when I was in my late twenties. That's when I started doing the bar bouncing thing. I wasn't making that much money. I was working for $40 a night, coming out of there bloody, with shirts ripped off my back. I couldn't even pay for the shirts. So I figured, *Okay, what I'll do is I'll take the civil service exam again.* Now—I don't want to sound insensitive, but at that point in New York, there was a protocol whereby you take the civil service exam, and if you are a minority, if you are non-white, you get 30 extra points.

MK: Well, there's nothing insensitive in it and this is just a fact. It's a fact of our law—

CML: They've been doing it for a long time. It's called affirmative action of course. And when that happens—I'm applying to be, let's say, a police officer, and all of these other guys, these non-white guys are looking also to be police officers. You learn that there's a line of three thousand guys in front of you, so then you give up your idea of being a police officer, and you give up your idea of ever succeeding, getting a job on the basis of a civil service exam. Now, they do have white police officers in New York, but almost all those guys are connected. They've got some kind of uncle or acquaintance or somebody who's on the police force that will put in a good word for them. I didn't have anybody like that, and merit made no difference whatsoever. This is not a meritocracy we live in. You can take any number of these tests and outscore everybody else and get nothing and nowhere.

MK: And it's especially true of civil service. It's true in a lot of fields in the economy, but especially in civil service, that has been a pronounced issue for a long time. So, presumably during all this time though, you're not just saying, as many people do when they leave college, whether they graduate or not, "Okay, well, that's it. I'm never reading a book again. I'm done with all that book learning." Something tells me that's not your mindset, even as you're doing these physical jobs.

CML: It certainly wasn't. And I would go to a library, sales—and found a little bookstore that had some academic books in it, and just get whatever I could. I always had to, basically, read whatever I found. I couldn't afford to order a book. Even back then, books were expensive. I couldn't go to a bookstore and pay full price for a book, so I was constantly buying used books, which were—when they were textbooks —used and therefore outmoded—the field advances, the book stays the same. But nevertheless, it's got some of the stuff that I need in it and then I can absorb that. So that's what I did. I just, basically, worked on my own ideas, trying to apply what I read in these books.

MK: Was there any field that attracted you in particular? I mentioned that I don't have anything past high-school math, and even that I was pretty sketchy on. Math, physics, philosophy, theology?

CML: Well, when I was fourteen, I was working on a ranch in Wilsall, Montana, which is just across Bridgers from Bozeman. I don't know if you're familiar with Bozeman, but anyway—I was punching cows, stacking hay, and irrigating on this ranch. I took two books with me. One of them was a book by Albert Einstein [Einstein, 1954] on the theory of relativity, and the other one was a book by Bertrand Russell [Russell, 1959] I would read these books—I was living in a covered wagon. They call it a sheep wagon these days, but literally—I'm not kidding—that's what it was: a kerosene lamp in a sheep wagon, out in the middle of a field.

MK: Reading Bertrand Russell and Albert Einstein—

CML: Reading Bertrand Russell and Albert Einstein, and it occurred to me, *These two things really need to be put together*. Then, once I decided that I started putting them together, and then I found out about Kurt Gödel and the undecidability theorem—and yes, absolutely. See, because reality isn't just geometric, which is what Einstein thought it was, nor is it just linguistic. It's a blend of the two. Russell saw it as being linguistic. Einstein saw it as being geometric. So I decided that reality must be logico-geometric, putting the two of them together, and of course, then I realized I've got to put together a theory—construct a theory in which reality is actually logico-geometric. That's where the CTMU came from.

MK: The CTMU is the Cognitive-Theoretic Model of the Universe. [Langan, 2002]

CML: The Cognitive-Theoretic Model of the Universe.

MK: This is your theory of everything.

CML: My theory of everything and it's all in the name. If you take a good, close look at that, you've got a cognitive theory, and of course, you know a theory is a kind of language, theoretic language. Then you've got a cognitive-theoretic model.

You've got a model, and then you've got a universe—you've got a language, you've got a universe, and then the model is the mapping between them. The CTMU says that those are all the same thing. All of those terms, all of those properties, are distributed everywhere over reality. Reality can have only one structure once you realize that and you implement it in theoretical form.

MK: So then, the question I asked you is kind of a stupid question, because I said which field was it that attracted you. And your answer is, "Yes."

CML: *(laughs)* Well, I would have to say it would have to be logic and language, and then physics and mathematics. So those are the fields, and that's what I thought I was conveying, but apparently I need to spell it out.

MK: You do! This is so important that you're not just talking about this siloed aspect of thought, or this philosophy over here, language over here, math over here, physics over here, but you are presenting something that is universal.

CML: Correct. Absolute and universal. To get the absolute invariance, the absolute truths of reality, things that are true everywhere you go, no matter at what time you exist, or in what place you exist—it's the same.

MK: So for those of us who have an IQ that's a little bit lower than yours—I'll admit it with no false modesty and no undue confidence.

CML: Well, IQ is not the last word on intelligence by any means. IQ is where you focus. You can focus, marshal all your intellectual energy, and focus it very tightly on one item that you've been presented with. Okay? Those tests contain items and you're focusing on each one of those items. You're not seeing anything else—and that's what IQ is. But in addition to that depth and that focus, there is also aperture. Think of the mind as a kind of camera. What a lot of high IQ people have a lot of difficulty doing is widening their mental aperture. You've got to be flexible. You've got to be able to widen and narrow that aperture at will as you're doing the depth perception too. So you've got the focus, depth of focus, the magnification as it were, plus the aperture. Most high IQ people, they have the magnification, but they don't have the aperture.

MK: So then from the perspective—simultaneously, I suppose, both of depth and breadth here—if we're talking about a theory of everything, the first question we have to establish: Does God exist?

CML: Yes.

MK: Simple as that.

CML: Reality has an identity. The identity is that as which something exists. As a matter of fact, when you say the word *reality*, you are naming an identity. You're identifying something. (*looks around and opens his arms*) This. [referring to reality]

MK: I'm smiling because your answer on this is so beautiful. It just reminds me of Moses at the Burning Bush, and Moses at the Burning Bush says, "Who shall I tell the people that you are?" talking to God, and God says, "Tell them, 'I am, that I am.'"

CML: That's right.

MK: I am Identity Itself. I'm Being Himself.

CML: That's exactly right and that's what the CTMU says. It just comes up with the mathematical structure that you need to build a reality out of. So you come up with that identity and then you search it for its properties. Once you've built the preliminary framework, then you start deducing the properties of this identity and you find out that those properties match those of God as described in most of the world's major religions.

MK: Just the theistic religions? I'm thinking of Judaism, Christianity, and Islam, or are you talking also of say—

CML: Buddhism, Daoism, Hinduism, Vedism. Of course Hinduism and Buddhism have a God. Daoism—their central principle is the Way or the *Dao*, and they don't see *Dao* as God. And then in Buddhism, of course, they are trying basically to achieve *Śūnyatā* or "emptiness." A lot of Buddhists don't even understand what that's supposed to mean, but once again, there's no God there—you can kind of read God implicitly. Some Buddhists—I've talked to Buddhists who actually think that there is a God in Buddhism of a sort. That concept of pure consciousness is what it is, and if you ask them, "Well, whose consciousness are you talking about?" they will point at themselves and say, "My consciousness." In a way they kind of attribute the existence of everything to themselves.

MK: I know a lot of people in Hollywood and Washington, DC, who do the same thing, actually.

CML: Well, that's right and that's why Buddhism is very fashionable among some of those people.

MK: (*laughs*) That's a good point.

CML: When you look at what they've all got, you come down to the same thing. Everybody has the *Dao* or the Way—that's the way reality works. Everybody has *Śūnyatā*, which is pure syntax—pure cognition with no instantiation, no content. Then you've got what the Abrahamic religions called God. It's all the same thing. But—what are its properties? Are its properties such that you can deny the existence of God, or are its properties such that God definitely has to exist? The answer is God exists. Properties of the central substance and central principle of reality, those properties are attributed to God, including of course things like—you have the three O's: omniscience, omnipotence, and omnipresence, but then you've also got consciousness—God has to be sentient.

MK: So we're not just defining God out of existence. Sometimes you'll hear people say, "God exists," but they'll give God such a weak and shallow definition that the God that they're describing has no relation to the God that we conceive of. You're saying God Himself is conscious and therefore personal?

CML: Yes. You can establish a personal relationship with God. We're images of God. You know what an image is—it's basically the product of a mapping. God maps himself into each human being. That's a very personal thing that God is doing for us. And I don't understand how anybody can say that it's any different. We reflect the structure of the universe, each one of us. We're carried by it, everything we do. We exist in a medium. What is that medium? Where did it come from? What holds it together? What is the unifying coherence, the source of coherence of that medium?

MK: Is your claim a pantheistic claim that God is the universe, or the universe is God, and that's that? Or no—or is God outside of the universe and created—

CML: God is greater than—well, what is the universe?

MK: Damned if I know.

CML: Have you ever heard of the simulation hypothesis?

MK: Yes.

CML: Okay. Well, the simulation hypothesis is basically the idea that the reality we see around us—physical reality—is simulated on some sort of an automaton or a computer.

MK: Yeah. Some aliens somewhere have just fooled us.

CML: Right, right, exactly—I'll eat a piece of liquorice.

MK: (*laughs*) Before one launches into the simulation, one needs a little sustenance, you know.

CML: The idea is that you've got some kind of an automaton running. You've got a simulation running on it. And God—it's more panentheistic. You know what panentheism is?

MK: I do. I think I do. That means that we are in God—let me know how I've gone wrong. We are in God and God is in us, and it is not merely that God in the creation are one and the same, but they are quite related. Is that something approaching panentheism?

CML: A little bit, yes. The idea is that you've got the physical universe that you see around you, but God is not confined to the physical universe. An ordinary pantheist thinks—assumes—that God is somehow confined to the universe, that there is just what we see around us and God is in every piece of it—God is distributed over it. But it's a little bit more complex than that because this part of the universe that we see around us, cannot exist just by itself. Okay? There are certain things that it entails. And when you go into those entailments, that's how you get to God. That's how you get to the identity of reality. Now, to get back to the reality of Self-simulation, or at least that's what I call it: Self-simulation. [Langan, 2020] But to get back to the simulation hypothesis, we are living in the display of that simulation. In addition to the display, there is also a processing aspect, and God captures both of those things. He captures both the display and the processor.

MK: What do you mean? I hate to put it in—

CML: Well, I mean, okay—here's the display. (*looks around*) You realize the display contains states. You see things, objects. States are static. That's why they're called states. Static. How do they change? Well, they have to be processed. Something has to be processing them, and in calculus, for example, those are tiny little infinitesimal intervals. But they're not actually contained in the states themselves. They have a neighborhood, a little tangent space or what have you, where you can sort of draw little vectors that suggest that some kind of processing is going on, but the idea of being a state and being a process, those are two different things in the ordinary way of looking at it. It turns out that you can't properly describe reality and causation at all, unless you put those things together somehow, and that's what it takes God to do. Okay? God provides the processing functionality for your state. You have an internal state and an external state. You're a material human being. To explain how that is changing through time and maintaining its coherence through time, even as it changes, that's what you need God for.

MK: I certainly agree with that entirely. I might not be sophisticated enough to parse all of the quibbles that there might be, but broadly speaking as a Christian, so much of what you're saying resonates as obviously true for me. The idea that, well, I'm a member of the body of Christ. The idea that God creates the world in this great act of love, this great act of charity.

CML: Self-love. Don't forget you're an image of God, so when loving Himself, God loves you, and you're supposed to love God back.

MK: Right, and this ties into something like the Trinity, right? The idea that God is three persons in one divine unity. So all of this is making a lot of sense to me. So now, how do I make sense of consciousness?

CML: Well, ordinarily—you know what quantization is?

MK: You know I know the word. (*smiles widely*)

CML: You decide what the ultimate irreducible objects are, those are the quanta in terms of which your reason. It turns out that in order to quantize that theory that I was talking about—that theory of identity where you've got the display, and you've got the processor, and it's handling both—it turns out that in order to handle both of those things, you need a certain kind of quantum. That quantum is called an identity operator. God is the identity, so obviously these little quanta, they're doing things, they're processing, so we can call them operators, right? They are identity operators. The identity operator, basically, takes input from the outside world, recognizes it, or accepts it using syntax, processes it, and then returns it to the world as an external state. So things come in, then they're processed, there's throughput—you could call that the subjective or internal state of the identity operator—and then it's returned to the external universe.

MK: But are you attributing now—

CML: What I'm saying is that's consciousness, and I'm saying that consciousness exists in every part of the universe, because those are the quanta.

MK: That's what I'm asking. Are you telling me that this table is conscious?

CML: In that sense? Yes. Generically conscious, but it's relying on our consciousness to do it. There's levels of quanta. These are tertiary quanta. They're all put together using physical localistic forces, but those are underdeterminative. They don't fully determine what happens. Why? The Heisenberg uncertainty principle, for example, tells you that the quantum rules are probabilistic, they don't actually determine events. So what determines events? We do. We don't know how we do it, but we do it. When everybody's will is put together, we're all creating the best possible universe we can for ourselves. And God is what harmonizes all of our different perspectives and makes things happen for all of us at the same time. And if we were doing things correctly, this would be the best of all possible worlds. Sadly however, we oftentimes make mistakes. And that's what we have to get out of doing, but we can't get out of doing it until we understand what reality is, what we are, and what the relationship between those two things is.

MK: Now you've mentioned two things that raise a new question for me. You mentioned this idea of simulation—just the simulation or Self-simulation—and you've mentioned us doing things. So then it would seem to me, we have to tackle the question, do we really do much of anything at all in the sense: do we have free will?

CML: Yes, we do.

MK: I'm glad to hear it. I always thought we did.

CML: Well, yes, we have to have free will. I was discussing with you earlier the idea of a fixed array—now, modern physics. Basically, you've got a bunch of quantum fields and superposition, and then those fields consist of little fluctuations, little quantum fluctuations, right? Where is the fixed array? We were talking about a manifold with a bunch of zero dimensional points, okay? Those two things are not compatible. Quantum field theory and that fixed array manifold, where you can parameterize all of the causal functions using the manifold: that doesn't work. Those two things don't fit together.

THE INTERVIEW

MK: When we were speaking about this earlier you put this into even more layman's terms and I've somehow—it has already flown out of my head. Can you put that into more basic terms? What you've just said.

CML: But what is it you need to understand about this?

MK: Why are these two concepts you're describing not reconcilable? What is the problem with these—?

CML: I explained that to you already. Alright. It consists of zero dimensional points, limit points, or cuts. I told you what a Dedekind cut was, right? These limit points have zero extent. They're exact locations, and that's a cut. You've got something on one side of the point, and then you've got something on the other side of the point, and any line that you draw through the point itself is going to be cut by the point. So we call that a cut. Okay? And the cut is zero dimensional, which means that it has no extent at all. It's an exact location. It's precise. No extent. It's not smeared out, okay? If you take all of those points and you add them together, you get zero. Because no matter how many times you add zero to itself, you just get zero. And because the manifold consists of those points, that's what you have to do to find out the extent of the manifold. So, what this is telling you is that the manifold itself has zero extent. There's nothing there. So the real manifold of classical physics is a paradoxical construct. Well, that's why that doesn't work with quantum field theory and the idea that things are quantum fluctuations and fields—as a matter of fact, that particular concept of the real manifold, that doesn't work for anything at all. It's a conceptual convenience. We can reason about reality in terms of it, and we can actually get to some very interesting conclusions using it, but it doesn't work in the long run. Most causal functions of course are parameterized in terms of this manifold. In other words, you've got the x, y, and z axis, and the forces that exist, that cause things to happen, those forces are all directed along one of those axes. That's what a force is. When you take away the points, those zero dimensional points, now, all of that disappears. The basis of causation has just fled the coop on you, right? Because you no longer have little points, the tails of the little vectors that point there, you can no longer parameterize your causal functions using those points and vectors. So what do you do to get causal functions? Well, it turns out you have to use something called advanced causation, and you combine that with ordinary retarded causation, and you get something else entirely. It's called meta-causation in the CTMU. It's referred to using two operations, one of which is called conspansion, and the other—sub-operation—which is called telic recursion.

MK: Because when we're talking about free will—often the conversation, especially these days, becomes this sort of shallow discussion of, "Well, this caused this, and I'm going to describe a totally deterministic system, and so as a result of this causing this, causing this, causing this, you don't have free will," and you're saying cause is actually more complicated than just—cause.

CML: That's correct. In other words, talking about free will on those terms was otiose—means nothing. You can't get anywhere with it. Reality is actually generative. It's not just a fixed manifold. Everything is being created all the time. Not just our states—our states are being recreated, right? I can cross my legs. I can uncross my legs. That's the changing state, but the medium around us is changing. When I look at you, I'm seeing Michael Knowles. I'm seeing you sitting there, but that means that I'm seeing your boundary. I'm seeing what distinguishes you from the external environment. There's a medium around you. So I have to be regenerating that at the same time as I'm regenerating your state in my head. Okay? And when I say regenerating—there's a reason I'm doing that—I could also say I'm recognizing Michael Knowles. I'm recognizing your state right now, but I'm also recognizing the state of the medium around you, because otherwise, I wouldn't be able to distinguish you from the medium, and you wouldn't exist at all.

MK: Right. Well, it's sort of like with a little baby that has trouble recognizing the limits of things and recognizing what some individual object might be—the glass on the table—they have trouble distinguishing those things.

CML: Precisely. The baby has to learn to distinguish those boundaries, and it has to receive the right visual cues at the right age, so that it can actually learn how to do that.

MK: So now we're at meta-causation. So what does meta-causation—how—?

CML: Causation works from past to future. Meta-causation works from past to future and from future to past, in a closed loop, it's called a conspansive cycle. Okay? So that's basically what we have to do to quantization in order to make causality wor—and of course, when I say causality, I mean meta-causation. Because ordinary past-to-future causality parameterized by a fixed array—that doesn't work.

MK: So I get past-to-future. This seems pretty simple. I pick up the glass of water. I put it over here, and now I remember two seconds ago that water was over here, and then I caused it to go over there. So how do you cause something to go from the future to the past?

CML: It can't go anywhere unless there's some place for it to go. That's all I'm saying. In the universe, everything changes with time. In the theory of relativity, for example, all the points are events and that means that there's a time parameter involved. So when you take that glass and you move it from there to there, you think that there's a point right there where you're going to move that glass. That's false. The point to which you are going to move that glass is actually in the future. When you pick up that glass, it's still in—you understand what I'm saying?

MK: Yes. Okay. That makes sense. And then getting back to God. Yes, we're always trying to get back to God. God is outside of time and space.

CML: God distributes over time and space, and there's some left over. Time and space is static. It's a display. Imagine that you're a little homunculus inside a computer display, like *The Matrix*, for example. Okay? God not only distributes over that, but there's a whole other domain where God exists, and that's the processing domain. That's the non-terminal domain in the CTMU. We're in the terminal domain. Right? And most physicists when they try to reason about the terminal domain, they reason under physical confinement: "Well, I can only look at physics, and I have to use what I know about physics, what I can observe about physics, to explain everything else that I explain." So they have that kind of explanatory closure going right there.

MK: So speaking of this non-terminal domain. In a really basic question—I'm not going to ask you if I'm going to go to Heaven or Hell, but will I go to either Heaven or Hell?

CML: You will persist after you die. Where you go, depends on who Michael Knowles really is (*both laugh*) and you would know that better than anyone.

MK: Yeah, I hope I know that better than—but you're telling me, I'm going somewhere.

CML: Yes.

MK: You're confident of that? I don't just evaporate. I don't just turn into oblivion.

CML: Well, you can. If you displease God, that's exactly what's going to happen to you. God is going to cut you off and He is going to say, "I can't see him anymore." He's going to turn away from you and then you won't be able to reunite. Salvation will be impossible for you because salvation means that God has got to pull you back into Himself. But God doesn't want to see you anymore. He doesn't even know you exist. He knows your physical body is there, but He's not interested anymore because you hate Him. You deny His existence, you offend Him, so He's not going to look at you, right? So now what happens? Well, you're dead. You still want to live. There's something in you that still desperately wants to live, so it's still going to be there.

What happens now? Well, you try to create your own world for yourself, but if you're a bad person, an evil person, what kind of world is that going to be? It's going to be an evil world, and that's what we call—Hell.

MK: This is what John Milton says in the mouth of Satan. He says, "The mind is its own place, and it can make a Hell of Heaven, or Heaven a Hell."[1] [paraphrase]

CML: Now you got it.

MK: It all reminds me of Dante, also. This idea of God turning away. At the very deepest part of hell is Satan frozen in a lake of ice of his own making because of the flapping of his own wings, because he's apart from the warmth of God.

CML: Precisely.

MK: Okay.

CML: That's the way it has to work.

MK: So we've gotten through death, judgment, Heaven and Hell, free will, and God.

CML: Not completely. There's a lot more to be said.

MK: And we still have some time. I mean, fortunately on my usual show, there is about thirty seconds to come to any conclusion about anything, and thankfully I am not bringing Chris Langan into Nashville to talk for ten minutes. This is going to be a much longer discussion. So—for this discussion, would you like a cigar?

---

1 "The mind is its own place, and in it self
  Can make a Heav'n of Hell, a Hell of Heav'n."

THE INTERVIEW

CML: (*laughs*) Sure, I haven't smoked a cigar in a long time.

MK: Oh, excellent. You know, the body is a temple. The temple needs incense.

CML: Back in the day, I used to enjoy a cigar every now and then.

(CLASSICAL MUSIC PLAYS)

CML: Good cigar.

MK: I'm glad you like it. This is one of my favorite cigars that's come out. You know, if you were on the Joe Rogan show, they would offer you something a little stronger, but (*Chris laughs*) we're going to keep it to tobacco on this show, I think.

CML: I think I've seen a couple of—yeah, I've seen the Rogan show a couple of times. He was talking about some kind of drugs. At that point in his career, I think that's all he was talking about.

MK: (*laughs*) Did you ever get into drugs? I'm not saying that just because you were around bars in New York, but even the drugs that everyone says expand your mind, and anything like that?

CML: Well, you couldn't really grow up in the era when I grew up, around the kind of people I was surrounded with, without trying some drugs—I don't have a substance abusive tendency in my body. I just don't have any bad habits except for this. (*reaches for liquorice*)

MK: (*laughs*) This is again liquorice and candy.

CML: Oh man, I love that stuff. It's addictive.

MK: (*laughs*) It is.

CML: But I have to hide it from myself. I don't have any in the house right now.

MK: So you never—because I would always have people tell me, especially in college, they'd say, "Michael, you have to drop acid. You have to smoke this. You have to take mushrooms. It's going to expand your mind," and I thought, *My mind—my brain, such as it is, is pretty much all I got. I'm not exactly the captain of the football team, and if some drug messes up my brain, I'm sunk.*

CML: That's correct. But of course, what they say is that some of these medications can actually be good for you in terms of—you may have certain things, certain mental routines that are destructive and that aren't good for you that can be interdicted by psychedelics, for example.

MK: What's your take on it?

CML: My take is that could very well be true. You know, the psychedelics could open up a gap between your temporal consciousness and your non-terminal consciousness, right? Your mind is an extended stratified thing. We're just using our terminal consciousness right now, but there are other aspects to your consciousness. You can actually get certain kinds of insights and communications if you just open up a gap. You understand? Let them come in and fill the gap and then you can see them as they would ordinarily—

MK: So the things that people see when they're on

THE INTERVIEW

psychedelics—I usually write them off and I tell people, "You are just hallucinating," but you're saying maybe that's not all it is. They might be seeing something real.

CML: Well, once again, what is reality? Is reality just stuff out there. No, reality has a mental aspect, right? And once you admit that basically everything has a metal aspect, then of course what's going on in your mind is real. It takes on a kind of reality. It's not the same as physical reality. It is nevertheless real.

MK: Are angels and demons real?

CML: Yes—yes.

MK: I think so too. Is there a fear that if you take some of these drugs, you might be letting in the wrong guys.

CML: That's a problem, isn't it? And that's a problem that I think a lot of people have encountered. You have to be a certain kind of person to be able to handle these drugs and not be sucked under by them, okay? Because once your mind is messed with in that way—it's weakened, you're not exactly in control anymore—something else can come in and grab it. And if you open up that gap that I was talking about, what can come into that gap might not be good for you.

MK: God is real. Angels are real. Demons are real. Is the Devil real?

CML: Oh yes. Yes. Well, it has to be. We were talking about Michael Knowles being surrounded by the medium—you've got a boundary. Well, God has a boundary too. He's got a very tight boundary. He's a perfect—He's perfect. He can't take anything resembling imperfection. He can't take it into Himself because that would be a contradiction, okay? So, God needs an antithesis in order to be properly defined. What is that antithesis? Anti-God or Satan. So it definitely exists. Now, Satan isn't coherent because he basically hates existence. Nevertheless, he gains coherence through human beings, through secondary telors as they're called in the CTMU. In other words, Satan can nucleate power structures, for example, things like corporations and governments, where you've got people in there that can be acquired as resources. And there's a kind of skeleton, a corporate organization, a governmental organization, that's holding them together, holding them in place, that can be exploited by Satan.

MK: So you're not describing Manichaeism. You're not saying there's God and the opposite of God, and there's some maybe equivalence between the two. You're saying that God—obviously there is an antithesis—Christ has an anti-Christ—but it's incoherent. Are you saying that the Devil sort of lacks substance, that's why he needs the humans?

CML: I'm saying the Devil lacks coherence. Coherence is what brings everything into superposition with itself. In other words, it allows—this is going to sound a little bit paradoxical—something to communicate non-locally with itself. All of its possible states are in superposition. They exist all at once. And this is pretty much inescapable.

MK: I'm reminded of a writer, René Girard, who had this idea that the Devil, being who he is, is a kind of contradiction of Being. And it seems to me what Girard says is something similar to what you're saying, which is that he requires us to kind of do his dirty work.

CML: That is correct, yeah. We give existence to the Devil, to Satan. Now, you have to make a distinction, however, between Satan and Lucifer, for example. Now, Lucifer is an angel. That's what he is supposed to—a fallen angel, but nevertheless, an angel, right? The angel of light, the morning star, whatever you want to call him. That is not Satan. Those are two different things.

MK: What's the difference?

CML: This would no doubt be classified as a heresy, for example, in the Church.

MK: I did not bring the inquisition with me yet. (*Chris laughs*) They're not behind the curtains here. So what is your idea then? Because traditionally it's understood that Satan and Lucifer are the same person. You're saying they're different.

CML: Yes. Yes I am.

MK: How are they different?

CML: Well, Lucifer walks the fence. Basically, he's the angel of light. What does light do? Basically light is what brings reality to us. He's walking the fence between good and evil. We're all in the same boat, we all walk the fence between Good and Evil. How can we do that? Well, through Lucifer—

MK: And the grace of God.

CML: —through Lucifer—basically Lucifer has been exiled

here because God can't take—won't tolerate the imperfections of this place. He has Lucifer handle that for Him, and that's why Lucifer is what he is. That's how he fell down here to Earth. He's performing a function here. That function is light. I mean—do you follow what I'm—?

MK: I do. I'm still trying to parse the difference a little. If Christ says, "I saw Satan fall like lightning from heaven," is he describing Satan here, or he's describing Lucifer, or both?

CML: If Christ were here and I could hear his exact words, I could perfectly interpret them.

MK: Right, okay.

CML: But it's very hard to do that two thousand years after the fact, with all the different translations and interpretations that the Bible has undergone. What I like to do is I like to approach it from first principles and look at it logically, rationally. And what does logic tell us, if anything? Well, logic tells us that basically God needs a negation, but that negation is too incoherent to function in this world except through human beings. What's the rest of it? What's the rest of it all about? Lucifer is a concept that is better suited than Satan to that purpose.

MK: I love this point that he's incoherent, that the old Devil is incoherent. I read some poem—I think it's a modern poem—that says sin is a big problem because it's evil, but it's also a big problem because it's such a waste of time. It's so incoherent. When you take the suffering out of it and you just think of people committing any particular sin, it just doesn't make any sense, does it?

THE INTERVIEW

CML: The sense that it makes to them is they're enjoying it. They're hedonistic, deriving pleasure from the sin. And of course we all, you know, have the same pleasure mechanisms, so we're all tempted to commit sin, but we've got to keep a lid on it. There have to be limits. And what I'm worried about is that now Satan controls the world, and there are certain people involved in running things, who don't have those limits. They're so rich, they're so powerful that they don't need those limits anymore. So they've more or less thrown them off.

MK: Now there's nothing new to the idea that Satan or Lucifer—or let's call him just the old Devil himself—is the prince of this world, and that the rich and the powerful do his bidding, and they're bad people, and they follow their lowest appetites and their pleasures, and they can be sadistic—so that's been going on for a long time. Is there something particular about the moment we are living in that says it's actually gotten much worse?

CML: Yes. We've had so many technological advancements that now the technology of surveillance and coercion are such—and these people are so rich—they're like black holes gravitating all the money to themselves—that they're unstoppable, and because they're unstoppable, because they actually run everything, we are endangered by them now.

MK: It sounds to me like you're saying we don't live in *Schoolhouse Rock!*—I'm a Bill up on Capitol Hill. We're not living in the Republic that a lot of us say that we're living in.

CML: That's correct. Basically the world is globalistic now.

It's run by globalists. That's their goal. That's what *global* means, "We're going GLOBAL." (*laughs*)

MK: That's oligarchic—and it would therefore be oligarchic.

CML: That's absolutely correct. Oligarchic, because very few of them actually exist.

MK: And this is beyond a US Senator. This is beyond the structures.

CML: Those are puppets. It's fairly common knowledge now, I suppose, that I regard most politicians as being one step removed from prostitutes.

MK: (*laughs*) That's been true for—they're two oldest professions.

CML: There are a few exceptions, but let me tell you, they're on the run. So it's a very serious situation. And if you take a look at these globalists, the ones that have thrown off all the limits, and they're fantastically rich and powerful now, and you take a look at what they actually have upstairs, I'm afraid it's not very impressive.

MK: Right.

CML: I mean if you really look at their intellectual produc—Soros might be the best of them. He's at least got a theory of economics. It's flawed, but he at least has that. The rest of them are just a bunch of sybarites.

MK: What about, I guess even outside of banking or finance *per se*, what about someone like Bill Gates? That guy's everywhere. He seems to be—I don't know why he is an expert on healthcare but my television tells me that he is, why is he—(*Chris makes a money gesture and laughs*) —so someone like that. But is he a—he's a smart guy. He's got to be, right?

CML: Oh, he's not stupid. Bill Gates has got a respectable intellect, but there's something misfiring there. Bill is very concerned with overpopulation and we do have an over-population problem.

MK: So then this brings me to—I asked friends of mine. I said, "speaking to Chris Langan, send in your questions," and most of the questions were about metaphysics, and God, and the CTMU, and all of your thoughts on all those things. But one friend of mine said, "You know, I want you to ask him about Bitcoin. I want you to ask him about money. Basically, if there is any way to break the government or super-government control of money." If I want to start my own currency I guess I could. I'd call it the Michael coin. Is this one way to push back against an increasingly techno-cratic global form of government?

CML: Yes there is but it has to start at the local level. You're not going to print your own world currency to compete head to head with these. You've got to go and basically attend a few city council meetings. You've got to go in there, say your piece, say, "We've got a problem: the world is run by globalists. This is America. We should have our right of self-determination here, but that's been taken away from us." See who agrees with you about it. Somebody will probably come up to you after your speech and say, "You know, I agree with you a hundred percent." Then you start—you find out who those people are, you get together, and you start putting pressure on your local politicians.

MK: Are you saying the situation is so bad, politically, that actually—people will call you a radical and an extremist and a terrorist for something like this—but are you basically saying, "Jefferson, we need to go fight another revolution or something, or is there—"

CML: I would just as soon see this whole thing resolved non-violently. Of course, I want peace on earth. I want everybody to feel as though we're in fellowship with each other—the Brotherhood of Man—you know what I'm talking about. That is the right way to do it.

MK: When you, or I, or Donald Trump for that matter, use the word *globalism*, what the liberal establishment will say is that globalism is good and we should have more of it, or they'll say that's a crazy conspiracy theory and there's no such thing as globalism.

CML: (*laughs*) What??

MK: I could point to a lot of international organizations that increasingly try to take power away from national governments.

CML: What are intelligence agencies? What are trade secrets? What's intellectual property? They're all property. They're all conspiracies, okay? People trying to get ahead by lying by omission, or lying directly to other people, the competition, right? That's what it is. You can't get away from conspiracy. It's how the world works, and—as a matter of fact—is game-theoretically rational.

THE INTERVIEW

MK: So you're saying not conspiracy THEORY, you're saying just FLAT OUT conspiracy.

CML: That's what makes the world go around, I'm afraid. Of course, the elite themselves realize this. They know that that's how the world works. They just want to distract you.

MK: Well, that's such a great way to put it, where you say a trade secret or just a group of people come together. They say, "I've got this good idea for a company, and we're going to come together and do that, and we're not going to let the competition know about it. We're going to start this and hopefully it'll be successful, and we'll make some money," and that is a form of—

CML: WEF and their young global leader program, young global leaders. I mean everybody's a young global leader, right? Trudeau, Macron, Merkel, Putin. For the Putin deal, that very much surprised me, but Klaus Schwab is on rec—he's on video, in fact, claiming that Vlad Putin is one of his young global leaders, trained in globalism.

MK: It's funny you mention the young wing of the World Economic Forum. When I was a freshman in college—you get all of these opportunities for internships and fellowships and you try to get a grant, and so you apply to these things. I don't know anything about any of these groups, and so I said, "I'm a politically-minded young man," very conservative, so it made me very different than my classmates, and one of the opportunities that came across was the World Economic Forum, *Global Changemakers* fellowship.

CML: You were invited to be a part of this?

MK: No, I applied. What did I kno—

CML: You actually applied?

MK: I applied.

CML: Shame on you.

MK: Well, I didn't know what it was. They said:

"What's the experience?"

"Well, I'm very involved in this conservative group and this right-wing group, and this—"

CML: Good way to get ahead. I got to give you that.

MK: Well, but I'll tell you, I thought I had a good résumé. It wasn't like my classmates. They had all their liberal groups. So I said, "I'm a conservative, but you probably want some conservatives here, right?" (*Chris laughs*) So I apply and, you know, you're going to be shocked to hear this, Chris. I didn't hear back.

CML: (*laughs*) Yeah, I'm absolutely flabbergasted.

MK: And my liberal classmates, who I felt had a weaker application, but they were all part of the liberal groups, they did get it. I guess it makes sense, now that I know what the World Economic Forum is.

CML: What is socialism? I mean, what is communism, right? These things were actually funded. They're more or less invented by the central ban—you know who originally was paying Marks and Engels, and before that Moses Hess, and other people to come up with—it's a strategy for world domination, and it has been for the last two hundred years. What has changed?

MK: So when someone like Trump comes along and he says, "I'm not going to fight this political battle along exactly left-right lines, or Republican–Democrat, but I'm saying I'm going to stand for the American nation, and nationalism generally, against globalism," but he managed to get through. He did get elected.

CML: Yes, he did.

MK: Were you a Trump supporter? You don't need to say if you don't want to.

CML: As a matter of fact, back when people were saying, "Trump can't read. Look at the way he hesitates. He's got trouble with the telepro—, the guy can't read." I actually stood up and I said, "No, I've met Donald Trump and I think his IQ is probably equal to that of the average Harvard professor."

MK: Really?

CML: Oh yeah. I actually stood up for Do—of course, I never got anything out of it, but I thought I was doing—you know, telling people that, basically, he is competent, he's a good businessman and therefore could be good for the country, and I wanted people to understand that.

MK: So how did this guy—I've asked this to my friends and I said, "How did this guy who I think was basically on the level, and really did at least try to pose a stopping block to the globalism program, how did he ever get elected? How'd they let him through?"

CML: Well, he was a little bit of a wild card, right? Trump is not as easily controlled as some of them are. So he stood up there and he spoke his mind. He's got good instincts in that respect because what he said resonates with what is in the minds of a lot of American citizens. We want to have our own country. We want America to have for us. We don't want our borders to be open. We don't want millions of third-world migrants coming here every year and displacing us from our own territory. And Trump actually did a good job of enunciating that. That's how he got elected. The first time around, you know, they weren't prepared, so they couldn't do anything about it. The second time around— (*laughs*)

MK: Are you suggesting, Chris, that there were some questions about the 2020 presidential election?

CML: (*laughs*) Anyone who doesn't understand that election was, shall we say, not quite up to snuff is some kind of moron.

MK: (*laughs*) Because I was told by all the fact-checkers, and all those social media censors that if I raised any question—I said, "You know, it seems like they kind of violated the law in Pennsylvania, and it seems like actually they kind of extended the voting periods. They said, "That's crazy. You're a conspiracy theorist. How dare you?"

CML: Well, that's exactly what they do. You see? You've

violated group-think, so you're out. Your opinion means nothing.

MK: How would you describe your politics? Populist, conservative—?

CML: I was always pretty much of an independent. When I was a kid, I was basically a democrat, working—my family was democratic. I think my stepfather was a—you ever hear of the Wobblies?

MK: Yeah, yeah.

CML: He was an organizer for the Wobblies out of Chicago. Always I was raised around this liberal attitude, so, yeah, we were democrats, and I thought, *Yeah, the working man, the people that actually hold this country together, that keep everything moving, those are the ones that we should really care about, and if we're not careful, the rich will walk all over them, so they need somebody to defend them and to take care of them.* I'm one of those people. I wasn't rich. My family had no money at all, so naturally I gravitated to that. Then the Democratic Party changed. No longer was it about the working man. Suddenly it was full of these billionaire techies that have never done an honest day's labor in their entire miserable lives, and I realized—wait a minute—things have changed here. There is no more Democratic Party of the kind that I used to know about, that I used to belong to, and that's when I became a conservative, and a conservative in a stronger sense than most people who call themselves conservatives today, because they're really just cuckolded by the liberals. (*Michael laughs*) They're afraid to say boo to them. I mean, look!

MK: You know what's funny? I was told, some years ago—this was probably 2016 or 2017—someone said, "Michael, you can't use the word *cuckold* as an insult because that's racist or sex—," and I said, "Look, I'm of Italian extraction and cuckold is the oldest insult in the Italian culture that—"

CML: The Sicilians have a gesture for that. (*laughs*)

MK: Yes. (*he extends his index and little fingers while bending the middle ones and the thumb*) And it's the rock-star gesture. I forget the name of the rock-star—also Sicilian who popularized it—very famous and I can't believe his name escapes me—but that sign is the symbol of the cuckold. I said, "There's nothing wrong about using it. It's a very funny insult and it's descriptive."

CML: Apparently, there are married couples that actually—that's their hobby. I can't see it myself, but—

MK: Not my thing. It's obviously—it's disordered. Nobody wants, you know—I don't think rationally anyone would say that's a good way to live your life. And what you're saying is that there are people who call themselves conservatives and really they're just squish, cuckolded, or they just give in.

CML: It's a figure of speech. We're not accusing them of literal cuckoldry.

MK: No, they might be, I don't know. I'm not in their bedroom.

CML: But basically they are letting the other party wear the pants, and they're putting on their little panties, and doing whatever they're told. That's what I'm saying. That's the modern rhino, the modern Republican, you know. I mean, that's what most of them are, and believe you me, most of them wouldn't do a damn thing for anybody else. They're basically into their own thing, their own self-interest. And they just never take any risks on behalf of the American people anymore. And that offends me—because we're paying them and they've promised to represent our interests and they're not doing it.

MK: Well, you look at really basic issues, something like immigration. Well, and Trump really won on the immigration issue. Something like immigration—this is no insult to anyone around the world who wants to come to the United States. Frankly, it's not even an insult to the illegal aliens who are pouring across the border. But I think anyone can agree, taking in one million legal immigrants, and two million illegal immigrants annually—it's going to be more than that this year probably—on top of that, three million people per year—

CML: Taking them in? Whose houses are they living in? You're see them living in anybody from Washington DC's house?

MK: No, it's not Martha's Vineyard. It's not Southampton.

CML: You don't see too many of them there.

MK: No, but it's a political strategy that is opposed. If you look at public opinion polls, the vast majority of Americans, including lots and lots of Democrats want to drastically reduce this immigration issue. And yet, doesn't matter which party gets elected, the border remains open. The West—especially after World War II, you've got this huge boom in the West. You've got the second half of the 20th century, now we're into the 21st century, that's where all the money is, that's where all the opportunity is, and so just naturally people want to flood in there, and if you've got relatively lax immigration policies—

CML: Well, in order to get into this country, you used to have to prove that you were of value, that you could offer it something. It wasn't just about us giving to you. If you were an immigrant and you wanted to come here, you had to show that you had something to offer yourself. Okay? You had to go through Ellis Island, or wherever, you had to learn English, you had to learn about the Constitution, you had to buy in to our political sys—

MK: But now it seems you're incentivized to hate America (*laughs*) or to hate Western civilization.

CML: That's right. And now who would be doing that? Any real American? Not that I know of. It's a contradiction in terms.

MK: So what's the end game here? I mean, if America—

CML: World domination. They're going GLOBAL. That's what it's all about.

MK: So, if we've got this oligarchic group, this self-appointed oligarchic group that I in my naiveté in freshman year of college, I say, "Oh, the World Economic Forum," or forget even WEF. There are other international organizations, the United Nations, obviously, the European Union, which the Brits have pulled theirselves out of. But there are these groups throughout the West that want to erase national borders, essentially.

CML: That's correct. And they want to deracinate everybody that lives inside.

MK: Yes, erase culture. I say this as the relatively mocha-skinned Southern Italian here. But there is a sense that—even just look at Europe. We don't want there to be French culture, and German culture, and British culture.

CML: I know. What a tragedy that is. Look at those cultures. They're beautiful.

MK: All the most beautiful cultures in the world end at the French, and the French on top of all those beautiful cultures too.

CML: (*laughs*) You know what the Brits always say, "France is much too good for the French."

MK: (*laughs*) Yeah. That's a good way to put it. So then what is your thought? Moving forward, we're in this very bad political spot right now. It would seem to me we've been in bad spots before—tower of Babel didn't seem particularly pleasant. The solution to that didn't seem particularly pleasant to live either.

CML: Divide and conquer.

MK: So what happens now? Do we just need to field a good candidate, or no, since it's too far gone for that?

CML: Well, the political system is kind of shot. Okay? So

I'm afraid it's going to take some activism. We're going to have to—look, I don't want anything violent to happen. I don't want a new revolution, but I will tell you this: that if people don't act as though they are willing to fight for their own rights, they're going to lose those rights. Founding fathers knew it, you know, it's written right into the constitution. If we don't fight for our rights, we're going to lose them—simple as that.

MK: You mentioned everyone getting stuck with the FaucI ouchie for the last two years, and, you know, it's so extremely effective that we all need to take 55 boosters too, (*Chris laughs*) just to marvel at the perfection and the efficacy of it. Are you anti-vaccine, generally? I take it you're anti-COVID.

CML: Well, I bought into the COVID thing, at first. And Gina and I bought gas masks for us—those N100 masks, and I advised people what to do, so as not to get infected with the deadly COVID. And then I noticed that, it wasn't really kill—I live in northern Missouri. Nobody up there was wearing masks and nobody was dying of COVID-19, so I realized, *Well, there's got to be something a little bit off about this, right?*, and so I kind of like started getting away from it, and then I noticed that it was being used as a pretext for something called the Great Reset.

MK: And again, I mean, to bring back the World Economic Forum, this is a page on the WEF website: the Great Reset of the Global Economies and the Global Political Order.

CML: Right. They're very open about it. Okay? And there have been white papers written in the past about using just this methodology to get everybody behind the globalist agenda, right? Operation Warp Speed was part of that, you know?

MK: So then, does Trump bear some responsibility for giving FaucI the microphone?

CML: He definitely bears responsibility. My question is: does he really know what's going on, or has he surrounded himself with people that are misleading him about what's going on? I would like to believe that Donald Trump has been misled, but if he knows how much damage those so-called vaccines have actually caused, and he's still pushing them, then we have a problem.

MK: You know, if you raise any questions about even the COVID vaccines, which at the very least, they don't do what Biden, and Fauci, and Walensky told us they would do, namely to stop you from contracting the virus or spreading it—at the very least, it doesn't do that—you're called a crazy anti-vaxxer.

CML: That's called cognitive dissonance, right? I mean, who's crazy? You know, if you can look at the reality of what is happening and you can deny it, and call anyone who believes in it, a conspiracy theorist, what kind of person are YOU? Well, you're obviously a nutjob, a kook, a moron. You're something like that, right? And that's what all these people are. As I say, "Conspiracy makes the world go around."

MK: Now, beyond finance or beyond these NGOs, you mentioned the intelligence agencies. Something that occurs to me is: if I were at working at an intelligence agency—they never invited me—never got that invite on ZipRecruiter.

CML: Perhaps you should consider yourself lucky. (*laughs*)

MK: (*laughs*) I think I do. I certainly do. But if I were at an intelligence agency and I've heard there was a guy with the highest IQ ever recorded who was contradicting the liberal establishment agenda, I'd probably have a file on that guy. Have you had any run-ins with the—?

CML: Some interest has been shown. It was oblique. They're very—let's just put it this way: I managed to meet three people that are involved in that line of work when there was no actual reason that that should have happened. In other words—but they're very cagey about it—if they want to recruit you, they'll probably do it obliquely. If you don't apply to actually join an intelligence service, but they're interested in you, they will try to get you involved with someone who they control, and then he will vector you around and put you in touch with the right peop—but you've got to accept the agenda sight unseen before that happens. Right? You've more or less got to let them know that, O*kay. No matter what they're actually planning to do, I'm going to go along with it, because I really, really want to be in the CIA*, or the defense intelligence agency, in the NSA or whatever. Right?

MK: No such agency.

CML: (*laughs*) There's no such agency, I like that. (*laughs*) Yeah, but you have to somehow display some sort of willingness before you will be directly approached by them. And

I guess I never displayed that kind of willingness, so I'm not there. I'm not in the intelligence community. I am, you know, periodically in touch with people who are in the intelligence community in various email distributions and things like that, but that's it.

MK: Since we're already in it, there are going to be people out there who'll say, "This guy is talking about every conspiracy theory I ever heard in the whole book." Since we're already in it, to take a slightly different tact, but still within the realm of what Wikipedia is going to call conspiracy theories—do you believe in aliens?

CML: Well, I will say this: the intelligence community, large sectors of it, believe in aliens.

MK: Really?

CML: Yes. Oh, absolutely. It's a big—I mean, they're constantly discussing these things. Yes. And if you look at the global elite, you know, and you want to—"Well, I don't want to blame the world banksters for this, that's a conspiracy theory." Then who is pulling all those strings? Could there be another kind of entity: aliens, demons, whatever. Could there be something that's pulling their strings—that the global banksters know about and they're taking orders from—but they're being totally concealed and hidden from the public? This is a viable hypothesis, and it's one that the intelligence communities don't reject—

MK: Hmm, it's funny you—

CML: —which is kind of neither here nor there, because the intelligence communities themselves could be run by aliens, for all we know.

MK: People are going to be laughing when you say that there are alien—

CML: Oh, let them laugh, but they won't be able to come up with any supporting argument against what I'm saying. They don't know enough. They're ignorant.

MK: It's funny that you mention angels and demons—pardon—aliens and demons in the same breath, because I don't particularly believe in aliens. I mean, what do I know? There are a lot of things I don't know about. But I certainly believe that demons exist. I'm pretty confident that demons exist. I'm less confident that aliens exist.

CML: Well, but the thing is a lot of people are reporting that they're seeing these UFOs, and other strange alien-suggestive phenomena.

MK: So what is—something like—they call it the Tic Tac: these weird UFOs that seem to violate the laws of physics.

CML: Correct. Basically they look like little blobs of light or spheres that can commit maneuvers that are totally against the laws of physics as we understand them. They look like they have mass, but somehow they're not subject to inertia. They can turn on a dime, on a right angle, and continue at the same speed. They can accelerate at tremendous g-forces. How can that happen?

MK: Do you have any theory?

CML: Well, yes I do, but it's an involved—it's fairly involved.

THE INTERVIEW

Basically, when you reduce the world to telesis and you understand that reality consists of a merging of mind and matter—it's an interplay of the two—

MK: It's not just stuff and it's not just pure abstraction.

CML: It can be real without necessarily being a completely physical phenomenon. Okay? In other words, there can be a mental component to it. Right? And that is what I think is happening here. I think that actually there's something to it. The number of people that report UFO incidents is simply too large. People aren't all liars. They don't run around risking their reputations by saying, "Okay, I'm going to make a nut out of myself and say these UFOs exist."

MK: But couldn't they just be nuts?

CML: Well, I suppose they could—

MK: But you're saying there is too many of them.

CML: I'm saying it's very improbable that they are, because not that many people are that nutty.

MK: You know, my friend Andrew Klavan who you met earlier, he has this party trick—he's a mystery writer and he has written ghost stories and things—and at dinner parties, he'll ask a random person, "Hey, have you ever seen a ghost?" and he says a lot of the time people will say yes. And throughout history people report having seen a ghost.

CML: That is correct.

MK: And he says, "You know, too many people are saying

they've seen a ghost for their not to be ghosts, or something like a ghost."

CML: That's correct. That is absolutely correct.

MK: Have you ever seen a ghost?

CML: I've seen things that look like ghosts—

MK: Such as?

CML: I've seen things that look like UFOs too. They're there. I mean, if you're not a very observant person, you'll never see anything like that. If your mind is completely closed, and you just screen all that stuff out, you'll never see anything like that. But if you're an open-minded person and you're observant, you will see things like that, eventually. Okay?

MK: Yeah. I don't want to put you on the spot to give an example, because if I describe an experience that I would call religious or numinous, sometimes people say, "Well, describe it." I can go around the edges, but it's somewhat ineffable. Could you describe such an experience?

CML: Well, yes, I could describe such an experience. On the UFO thing, I was working for the forest service near Lewistown, Montana, in the Lewis and Clark National Forest, not too far from Malmstrom Air Force Base. And I was in charge of a mountain range called the Little Snowies. I was the regional fire guard for that area, and I was alone up there. There were campgrounds and I'd go up and tend to the campgrounds and make sure that they were all cleaned up and everything, and that was one of my duties. And I had to be a fire guard, which means spotting and putting out forest fires and things like that. One day I was up there in a forest service pickup truck at a certain campground. I was there and suddenly—I look up—and I say suddenly—it was just in the sky. I became aware that it was up there and I looked up. It was this huge spheroidal, but elliptical, not a perfect sphere, like a saucer that was turned partially on its side. And I thought, *Well, that must be one of those lenticular clouds that I've heard of*, so I looked at it and I figured, *Okay, now I wonder how this evolves in time.* Totally changeless. I actually took sticks and I tried to use parallax to figure out, you know—*what is this thing? Why isn't it changing? Why isn't it moving? Why is it completely featureless and metallic looking?* Well, it wasn't any lenticular cloud. I literally stared at it for a long, long time before I finally just got, *Okay. It's there.* I got back in my pickup and drove away.

MK: Did you call it in or anything?

CML: I've told a number of people about it. Yeah. I didn't call it in. No, it was irrelevant to the state of my campgrounds, you know?

MK: It's funny you mentioned because—sometimes people say—this is a little different than seeing a UFO, but somewhat related—people will say, "I don't believe in God. I don't believe in Christianity because I don't believe in miracles. If miracles really happened, we'd all know about it, and—" One, if you look at the gospel accounts of miracles happening, the wildest part of it is not the miracle happening. It's the fact that when the miracle happens, everyone treats it as this miraculous event, and then five seconds later, they move on and people treat it as totally ordinary. And this happens again and again, and again, it's even happened—I would say that I've experienced things that are miraculous.

CML: Yes.

MK: And even in my own life, not one week later, I'm just going about my business as though it never happened. Or I'll forget that it happened or anything—it was a miracle! Shouldn't that—?

CML: But you don't deny that they happened?

MK: No.

CML: Right.

MK: I don't deny.

CML: That's the important thing, because then you know, you're really nuts.

MK: Yeah. (*laughs*) When you deny that it happened, right?

CML: That's right.

MK: Because you're so beholden to some preconceived notion of the way things are.

CML: That's correct. So, who are the real nuts? Obviously, they're the people that are doing all the talk about the alien conspiracy theories. Okay? There's obviously something there, or the number of people that report them wouldn't be reporting them. There are people in the CIA who actually claim to have been abducted. I'm not going to tell you who they are, but they're there. Okay? And we're not talking about small individuals. We're not talking about low-ranking individuals. We're talking about high-ranking individuals.

MK: These people—not just that you've read a book about—you're saying these people you've talked to.

CML: People that—there was one of them in particular that I was actually—somebody that I knew was trying to arrange an introduction to this person, and I said:

"Well, so he's in the CIA. Is he going to tell me the truth? I'm not in the CIA. Is he going to tell me the truth about anything?"

"Well, no, actually what he wants to talk about is abductions, because, you know, he and his wife were actually abducted by aliens and he wants to talk to you about—"

"Is he going to tell me the truth about anything?"

"I don't know."

"Then I don't want to talk to him. I don't want to talk to him at all. There has to be some kind of understanding that I'm not going to get lied to. Otherwise, I'm wasting my time, because I'll never know whether he is lying or telling the truth."

So if somebody isn't going to commit upfront to telling me the truth, I don't have time for him.

MK: If he were a really smart liar, he would've just said, "I will tell you the truth," and lied even if he wanted to.

CML: I suppose so. I mean, that's what they do in the CIA.

MK: Yeah. It's sort of the job, right? If you're a spy—

CML: That's correct. Than you lie your ass off at every available opportunity about everything. They don't all do that. I think there are a couple of people that I sort of trust when they talk about certain subjects. But by no means are they entirely in the know even. I mean, if you're in the CIA, you're basically a bureaucrat. You look up, you see— "Well, I've got my superior and then I'm looking up farther. Now, I see the director of the CIA—" Who's giving that guy his orders? It ain't the president. I mean, suddenly you're in a void. Who's running things? As far as most of these guys are concerned, it could be the Devil himself that's running things. They just don't know.

MK: You know, it's so amazing that you say that because it takes it full circle to the point that when I hear, "Okay. This so and so is actually really beholden to so and so, and this person is actually beholden to this person—", and I know that that's a fact because you can just see it in politics. You can actually kind of go to an org chart and kind of point to it, but then eventually say, "And so and so, if in a really powerful position, they're actually responsible to so and so, and accountable—", and you think, okay, at a certain point, you think, *I don't know. I have no way of verifying this. This could be it*, and then when you go all the way back to "and so and so is really just answering to the Devil." Now you've got me again, because I read that in my Bible. I know that that's true. I know that he is the prince of this world.

CML: Well, yeah, yes. By the way, I mean, there are accounts from biblical times and pre-biblical times that involve UFOs, things in the sky that show up during critical battles, for example, and turn the tide, right? This goes all the way back to the Vedic religion, the pre-Hindu religion. There are all kinds of people who have reported these things and they end up in various religious scriptures, including Christian scriptures as well, in some cases.

MK: I can't think of an example of an extraterrestrial appearance.

CML: Well, no, they're basically attributed to God. These are the interventions of angels or something. You even can go back and look at the Mayans, and the Incas, and people like that. There are pictures on temple walls—rather they're carvings—that seem to suggest that these things actually existed or at least were perceived.

MK: Right. There is a great meme that I'm really taken with—it actually has to do with IQ, which is a nice coincidence, but I love this meme, because it's got the really stupid guy at the one end of the bell curve and he is sort of drooling, and he says, "Duh, all the bad stuff is because of the Devil." Right? And then you get up on the bell curve into—I don't know—say IQ of a 120 or a 130, and it's the really smart guy, the egghead with the glasses. And he says—

CML: No, that's just the start of the danger zone.

MK: The danger zone: when you're just smart enough, but not smar—and those guys, they say, "No, actually the Devil doesn't exist, and actually we're all just sort of bags of chemicals and it's all rationally explainable," and blah-blah-blah-blah-blah—and then you get up to the guy at the really high end of the IQ curve in this meme, and he says, "No, actually the bad stuff's just from the Devil." He agrees with the guy at the other end of the— (*laughs*) but it strikes me that there's really something to that. Roger Scruton, the late conservative philosopher, said that the job of the conservative intellectual is to articulate things that the common man knows intuitively.

CML: That's right.

MK: And it's especially interesting when it comes to you, because you're a guy at the very highest end of the intelligence spectrum, and you've lived the life of a blue-collar guy.

CML: That's right. I wanted meaning in my life. It's like I say, I wanted meaning above all things. You got to make sure that you decide upfront when you're a young man, if you want to accomplish anything—who do you serve? Truth or Mammon? You don't have a choice—you do have a choice, but you can't do both at once. It's either going to be truth, which is the same as God—I mean, truth and God are to some extent synonymous—

MK: Yeah. The good, the true, and the beautiful.

CML: —or it's going to be money. And if you choose money, if you choose Mammon, then you're going to be serving Mammon, who happens to be the globalists at this point, because they control all the wealth and power.

MK: So, you mentioned—I think we totally agree Marxism is a very terrible ideology that's caused a lot of suffering in the world. You would agree.

THE INTERVIEW

CML: I'm not wasting this cigar.

MK: Absolutely not. Take your time, please. But so, we would agree with that: we're pretty anti-Marxist. Yes.

CML: I'm very anti-Marxi—it's a terrible philosophy. I mean, it's as full of holes as you can imagine.

MK: Even though all the geniuses at Princeton or whatever—there's all these Marxists.

CML: Look, that's a closed—that's a club. If you don't have the key to the clubhouse, you're not getting in. They won't even talk to you. No academic will take me on—will actually start arguing, even in his own field at this point, because they know they're going to lose, and they will. Any academic anytime.

MK: I'm as anti-higher-education cartel as there can be—

CML: Right. They're indoctrination mills. You have to look at the entire educational system as being one great big indoctrination factory, and the people that work in it—those faculty members—they're chosen, they're selected as indoctrinators of the youth.

MK: Yes. And they pedal Marxism. But I like what you just said. You boiled it down even more simply. A lot of politics comes down to, "Well, you are a socialist and I'm very anti-socialist," and "Well, you're a capitalist," or this or that. But you seem to be raising some problems with capitalism. Man cannot serve two masters.

CML: Well, there are two kinds of capitalism. One of them is, laissez-faire capitalism: you're supporting your family,

57

you're trying to get ahead, you're trying to enjoy a good and comfortable life, but you're not forgetting about God, while you do it. Then you've got monopoly capitalism, and this is what libertarians and other people sometimes forget: that laissez-faire capitalism. Because money gravitates—it's like a black hole—it takes money to make money. You got to have a bunch and once you have a bunch of it, it comes more and more easily to you—I think you're out of butane.

MK: I know. (*trying to light a cigar*) Let me see if I can will—there we go! Hey, how about that? Not quite miraculous, but good. So, monopoly capitalism is the sort of thing we call crony capitalism, crooked capitalism, but it's—

CML: Basically, you're not just controlling the supply side, you're controlling the markets. Okay? You're told what you can buy: "We've decided that everybody should be using electric cars. We're not going to sell the other kind anymore." That's monopoly capitalism, and because if you control the manufacturing, the industry, right? If you're a trade organization or a trade association and you control that industry, you can literally control the market. You can only buy what you have the opportunity to buy, what they're giving you the opportunity to buy. These days, they're only giving you what they want you to have. Those are the only choices you have as a consumer.

MK: They're doing this with light bulbs to it. It drives me nuts. They tried to do it ten years ago. They are trying to ban incandescent light bulbs, which I find to be much more beautiful than those ugly LED, or any of the other light bulbs. I just—in my home, I just find it's warmer and more beautiful to have, and they are trying to outlaw.

CML: Well, my wife agrees with you.

MK: Really?

CML: Well, we have those old-style incandescent bulbs in the bedroom, for example.

MK: I think of my Christmas tree. I don't want those little LEDs. They're harsh. They're ugly. They're blue. I want the warmer light and yet—

CML: But they do make LEDs, by the way, and almost all frequencies these days. You can get daylight LEDs. That's costly though. I mean, they're way more expensive than an incandescent bulb.

MK: So, this actually raises even a different question here. We've talked about truth. We've talked about goodness. There's one more transcendental: beauty.

CML: Correct.

MK: Where does beauty factor into your thoughts about everything?

CML: Well, here we get into the CTMU—we all know about the monetary economy, right? You get money, you buy things, you increase your wealth. The economy is actually telic. It's a vast favor-bank. I do for you, you do for me. This is actually the trading system that exists in nature.

MK: Can you define the word *telic*?

CML: Yes. *Telesis* is the monic substance of which everything else is composed.

MK: Okay, I think I've got it.

CML: In other words, some people—a physicist says, "Well, that's energy. Energy is the basic substance of which everything is—", mass-energy, right? I'm saying, "No, you've got to go up a step." You need something more general with other properties that, for instance, can accommodate information. You need something more general than energy to explain that. Or, if you want to, you can play a little semantic game and then expand, gradually, the definition of energy, so that it takes everything in. But I call the ultimate extension of that telesis. Basically, it's a fundamental form of intentionality. And if you want to talk about the intentionality of God, then you're talking about a dirty word in academia and what is that? Teleology. The Will of God.

MK: Right. The things have a purpose.

CML: That's correct.

MK: Yes. And so you're saying that there is this telic aspect to the economy, too.

CML: That is fundamentally the ONLY aspect. Money is an abstraction of that. It's a very specified, controllable, physically-commoditized version of telesis, and you have a certain group, a certain crowd that has established a monopoly on that. Now, when you establish a monopoly on money, you're actually monopolizing the telic economy as well. How? People invest their telesis in what can make them money. Unless you're like me and you prefer meaning in your life.

Truth. All right? That's what telesis is and it encompasses not just money, but truth and meaning.

MK: That the way that money and the monetary economy is manipulated will take into it many more aspects of life that—and maybe steer them the wrong way—let me try and bring it to Earth, at least in the way I was thinking about it, which is: I HATE modern buildings. I hate them. They're so ugly.

CML: Drab and Soviet style.

MK: They are. And they bring me down, and I walk into Grand Central, a nice old building in New York, and I feel like a king, and I feel dignified, and I feel like a full human being, and then I walk into tha– they've actually recently tried to make it better, but—

CML: Imagine how you'd have felt in the Notre Dame cathedral before they burned it down.

MK: Which I never got to see. I never got to go in.

CML: Me neither.

MK: So, what is that experience like? I wonder for someone who's just got this perhaps quirk of birth, where you just have this extraordinarily high IQ, what is the experience of life? Is it kind of funny and amusing, or is it extremely annoying?

CML: I hope somebody got a little charge out of it, got a little amusement out of it, because I sure as hell didn't, most of the time, but I don't complain. This is God's a world. God gave me my lot, knew that I was going to go after meaning instead of money, and everything that came after was more or less like clockwork.

MK: If you had any say in the matter, which you don't, and in which you certainly did not, would you choose to be born very intelligent or of middling intelligence, or of low intelligence?

CML: What do you think the answer is? I wouldn't trade my mind for anyone else's. Nobody. Simply because I know, I understand what the difference is now. If you're not intelligent, you don't cultivate your intelligence and make the most of it, eventually you lose sight of truth entirely, and that's what has happened to most of these people. They're adapting, you know? "Okay. We've got a narrative. I'm not going to get ahead in life, unless I accept the narrative," so they accept the narrative. It's called adaptation. It's artificial. It's not like natural selection where nature selects you. You're being selected now by a bunch of ideologues, bunch of people who want you to adopt a certain way of looking at things, because they have all the money and power, and they want to keep it forever. That's why the Christian Church has fallen so radically out of favor with most of these people, even among certain Christians, high-ranking Christians, all right? It shows up in everything they say, and I don't want to mention any particular Pope, on the other hand—

MK: You're referring to a certain Mr. Francis, present Vicar of Christ? Well, he says these things that are so puzzling and potentially heretical, and certain cardinals have raised dubia—doubts—and said, "Could you please answer this? It sounds like you've said something heretical." And the answer is always (*imitating an Italian accent*), "Well, you see, the Papa was'a misunderstood. He was'a misinterpreted (*Chris laughs*) in *la Repubblica* newspaper." And you say, "Well, you know, if he keeps being misreported and misinterpreted, why does he keep giving the interviews to these atheists and far leftist journalists?" I don't know. It's not mine to answer, I guess.

CML: Exactly. And I mean, this is something that I think needs to be addressed by the Catholic Church itself, if it wants to stop shedding Christians, right and left, you see. Because people are not stupid. I mean, some of them can convince themselves of things that aren't true, but basically human beings are intelligent. And you're cheating your intelligence when you subscribe to these narratives, and apparently the Pope who communicates directly with God, he buys into these narratives and that's a contradiction in terms.

MK: You know, it's funny you mention Papa Francesco because he's come after the Latin Mass and a lot of young—

CML: Do you know he claims to have been a bouncer at one point in his life.

MK: I read that somewhere. He doesn—you know, you look like you could be a bouncer. Papa Francesco does not look like he was a boun—I don't know. Do you buy it?

CML: (*laughs*) Maybe in a really light-duty nightclub, he might have made it, you know what I'm saying? Certainly not in most of the ones that I worked in.

MK: He's gone after the Latin Mass, and I've noticed that young Catholics—you know, I fell away. I was basically an atheist for about ten years. Something that drew me—there were a lot of things that drew me back—but something that drew me back was the Latin Mass and specifically the beauty, the smells and the bells, and the idea that the priest is facing the altar, and we're all facing together, and he's leading us in our worship of God. And it's not just acoustic guitars and feel good and be a nice person, and making it all about us.

CML: It's the sense of the sacred.

MK: The sense of the sacred and a sense of the beautiful. It's why I ask that question about the role of beauty in your ideas.

CML: That's once again a function of the telic-economy. Basically, it's synonymous with teleology. Something cannot be anti-teleological or deviate from the Will of God and still be objectively beautiful, all right? I mean, there are people who who can take a religious icon or a picture of Jesus Christ, for example, and urinate on it, like Larry David, I mean, I don't know.

MK: Or even there was the famous picture *Piss Christ*, right? It was a photograph of a crucifix.

CML: Isn't that disgusting?

MK: Disgusting. It was funded by the federal government. I think it received funding—

CML: They paid for that?

MK: I believe it received some amount of funding from—I could be getting this wrong, so don't quote me—but I thought it was the National Endowment for the Arts, or one of those organisations.

THE INTERVIEW

CML: Really??

MK: I could be wrong, but—

CML: That's bad, real bad. So—I don't know what to say in defense of these people. I don't think there is a defense for them. But if that's the kind of thing that they regard as art, then they are not in touch with beauty, and the reason they're not in touch with beauty is that they're not in touch with truth.

MK: But I thought—I was told by all my modern teachers that beauty is in the eye of the beholder. It's a subjective thing, and it's not objective.

CML: It is. But unfortunately some beholders leave something to be desired (*Michael laughs*) in their aesthetic sense.

MK: You're saying there is an objective standard.

CML: Yes. Absolutely. Is it consistent with teleology or is it not? Obviously—basically you've got this identity—God—who is perfection. Anything that deviates from that cannot, by definition, be good or beautiful. Now, nature experiments. I mean, it goes from one thing to another and tries certain things out, but once it becomes evident that something isn't working then it's not consistent with teleology. Once it proves to be degenerate and causes people to become demoralized and sick of life, then we have to do away with it.

MK: I've been told that we need to tolerate all sorts of—

CML: God does not tolerate evil and neither should we.

MK: It's a beautiful way to put it. So what do you make of the modern right? You know, the modern left is always pushing this stuff, but a lot of the modern right says—there was a prominent columnist who called himself conservative. I guess he sort of was for a while, but now he's pretty firmly on the left, and he said, "I don't like Drag Queen Story Hour, but we need to tolerate it, it's one of the blessings of liberty. If we don't tolerate drag Queen's story hour—"

CML: What?? A blessing of liberty?

MK: Look, it's in the preamble to the constitution. I think James Madison's rolling over in his grave at the very thought of that—

CML: Constitution mentions trannies, does it?

MK: Not in my last read.

CML: I was raised in an environment where we were basically taught to be tolerant of people, of their foibles, and if they wanted to be a little bit deviant—well, a little bit of deviation is good. You know, you can't just be locked into one rigid way of looking at things, so I developed tolerance, but now they've become militant. They've become rabid. They're shoving it down children's throats, and it's just not good for society. It violates the biological imperative of survival. To become totally sexual—there's a reason that men and women exist, and that they mate, and create children. It's for the survival of the human race. That has to remain paramount. That's got to be the preferred mode of existence. You've got to buy into that. Now, if you want to be—if you want to deviate a little bit in your private life, and you've got somebody who agrees to be deviant along those lines, and you want to get together in the privacy of your own abode that's—

MK: You're not going to have Chris Langan knocking on their door.

CML: I'm not going to knock on their door. It's none of my business. It's for them to work out with God Almighty, and if they can do that, more power to them. I don't know how they're going to do it, but give them a chance, okay? But when they go out and they have gay day parades where they're cavorting nude, and they're going into children's restrooms, and so forth—that's where we have to draw the line, you see?

MK: I mentioned this modern writer who is very misguided on this particular point. Are there thinkers alive today who you think are worth reading? People always say, "What's the reading list. What should I read? What should I listen to? Are there philosophers or popular writers—?"

CML: There are no academic philosophers that are worthy, as far as I'm concerned, of attention.

MK: What about non—?

CML: It's not because all of them are stupid or anything like that. It's because they bought into the party. They're academics. They cannot violate the academic, communistic, atheistic narrative, and get away with it. And if you're in that system then obviously you're playing along with it, and you can't do that and be an honest, truthful philosopher.

MK: Are there non-academic writers, thinkers, philosophers, who you would recommend people read?

CML: I'm sure they're out there. I haven't encountered any, not recently.

MK: So that gets rid of the living people. What about those dead guys, all those old dead guys, going back to ancient Greece, or anywhere in the middle?

CML: Oh, a lot of those guys had something very useful to say. (*smiles*)

MK: If a listener right now said, "I want to know who, beyond his own writing, the smartest man in the world wants me to read." Who would you recommend?

CML: Well, I would say that you should go back and definitely read Aristotle, and Plato, and Socrates. Start with that and then go up, and then work your way through there. A lot of smart guys read Plotinus, read about neoplatonism, and once you find out about neoplatonism, then you can go back to the ancient Vedic religion, because it's basically the same thing in different language. And as you know, then neoplatonism kind of became a mainstay of medieval Christianity, and there's a lot to that. So that takes us up through some of the medieval Christian philosophers: Aneslm, Aquinas, Augustin, and beyond that it starts getting dicey. I mean, even when you get up to like René Descartes, for example, everything becomes dualistic. You've got these Cartesian spaces that more or less exclude the observer. There are no images of God in a Cartesian space.

MK: Chris, have you ever—because you worked at

THE INTERVIEW

bars—you ever hear about the horse who shows up to the bar and asks the bartender for a drink? And the bartender says, "Horse, man, you've been here every night this week, I think you're an alcoholic," and the horse says, "I don't think I am!" Poof! The horse disappears. Now you see, you will understand this. This is a joke about Descartes, who says, "I think, therefore I am," but if I had told you that part first, I would've put Descartes before the horse.

CML: (*bursts out laughing*) I like it!

MK: This is the only successful circumstance in which that joke has ever landed. I'm really pleased. I finally got a laugh out of that joke.

CML: That's a very intelligent joke. Much more intelligent than the ones I usually hear.

MK: Well, thank you.

CML: Especially in a bar.

MK: (*laughs*) That at least I can believe. So, that digression aside, I'm glad you bring this up because people always ask me—they say, "What philosopher should I read?" I say, one, "Why are you asking me?" but two, they always say, "Should I read John Locke? Should I read Rousseau? Should I read John Rawls? Should I read this?" I say, "Maybe focus a little earlier first." And it's funny you mention: once you get up to Aquinas, after him things start to go a little like kooky.

CML: A little south. Until now, of course, all of that is completely out of fashion, and most of these modern philosophers are really Frankfurt-school-type people and that's cultural Marxism, which of course is just the social program of the Marxists.

MK: But, Chris, even though I just wrote a book last year on cultural Marxism, I have been told, reliably informed by Wikipedia, that's just a crazy conspiracy theory.

CML: Yes. Well, Wikipedia seems to think I'm a crazy conspiracy theorist too. You read my biography there?

MK: (*laughs*) Not recently.

CML: Everything bad that you can say, you know? Basically, I was exiled from Wikipedia years ago. I went in and said, "Now, wait a minute, here. No, I'm not an intelligent design creationist *per se*. I have a different approach to teleology," and all that, and I was immediately kicked off Wikipedia. So I can't—they can say whatever they want to in my biography in Wikipedia. There's not a thing I can do about it.

MK: Because you even suggested the idea of some sort of intelligent design.

CML: That is correct. Well, I've been getting trolled ever since around the year two thou—that goes back further than that really, but when I went on national television and said, "Well, the existence of God is actually amenable to logical analysis and you can show that there is a God provided you have the right—" That was enough: "Intelligent design creationist, get out of here." You know, and these people are—by the way, these new atheists, I mean, they're adamant.

MK: You're talking about Richard Dawkins, Daniel Dennett.

THE INTERVIEW

CML: I am talking about Richie Dawkins, Daniel Dennett, Sam Harris—well, I don't know, Chris Hitchens. I mean, guys of this nature, you know, pyz Myers—PZ [Paul Zachary] Myers, and people like that. I had a run-in with Myers. I mean, he hates my guts. He hated my guts twenty years ago. None of them will mention my name now though, because they know that they can be crushed. Deep down inside they know—they won't come anywhere near me. At some point, these people decided that they had to exclude anybody who could beat them. That's where the cancellation thing began, really. It's a new-atheist thing, and now since the new atheists are a lot more fashionable than Christians are, that's the order of the day.

MK: I blame my falling away from the Church on just being a punk 13-year old boy, but the second thing I blame is the new atheists. They were very popular at the time and I was very taken with them. Chris Hitchens. He's a funny guy. I thought, *Okay, he must be a smart guy.*

CML: Excellent speaker, incisive, witty, but obviously he just hates God. I mean, he makes that very clear: "All religions are evil because they mislead people and drag people away from—"

MK: But you didn't just say that he doesn't believe in God. You said he hates God.

CML: Hates God. Dawkins obviously hates God. "Why is there evil in the world?" usually. That's what it comes down to. "Would a just God tolerate all of the evil that is occurring in the world?" The fact of the matter is there can be no good—there can be no pleasure without pain, there can be no good without evil. God knows that there is always the possibility to commit evil—

MK: Free will, right?

CML: Right. But he has given us free will. He bequeathed that—we're his images. He is free. Therefore, we are free, and he expects us to fight against evil, to stop it from triumphing.

MK: Then, given will, and the fact that you use these words hate and love—very often when people talk about God, it's as though it were some academic exercise, "Well, do I believe in God, do I—", but you're using verbs that are more active than that—

CML: Yes.

MK: —hate and love. Do you think that our discussion or our understanding of God therefore must be active and participatory rather than merely academic?

CML: Absolutely. And furthermore, it must be rational as well as faith-based. Lot of religionists are fideistic, which means they rely completely on faith, and say that we can have no knowledge of God. Wasn't that nonsense? You have to know what you got faith in. How can you invest faith in something that you don't know what it is? You need at least an elementary description of it before you can predicate—before you can attribute faith to it, before you can invest belief in it. If you invest belief in X, but you don't know what X is, is that meaningful? Obviously not. So faith and rationality are indelibly coupled. There's just no other way to talk about it. So as soon as you hear somebody

THE INTERVIEW

say, "Well, it's entirely a matter of faith and we can believe whatever we want to—have faith in whatever we want to," that makes no sense at all to me.

MK: I totally agree with that, and it does bother me when religious people speak in that way in modern times. It's funny though you mentioned Thomas Aquinas. Was there ever a more rational guy in the world than Tom? The guy who wrote—to every question in religion, he had three objections and then answers to the objections. Quite a rational—

CML: We've gotten to another Aristotle. But all of these early-Christian philosophers are now out of fashion. Nobody pays attention anymore—well, except Christians, real ones, not fake ones.

MK: Practicing ones.

MK: So then—I know, I've kept all of your time, but I don't care, darn it! You're here in Nashville and I've got—

CML: Yeah, I'm just fine.

MK: Do you have religious practice?

CML: There is—yes. Well, let's just put it this way: I don't currently attend church but up until several—I started doing, like, my own kind of thing with preaching, right? So I decided that I didn't—but I was for about 10-15 years—I went to a little country church up the road from us. I live on a road where there used to be three historic churches. Two of them were burned down. Arson.

MK: Not accidental.

CML: Not accidental, no. And they were historical Civil War era churches, but one was left. And it was north of us, about two and a half miles north of us, on route P there. So I attended that church pretty religiously, very regularly for a long time. Now, as it happened, the last thing that I heard—it's run by a wonderful lady that actually takes care of most of what goes on there, and it's got a good pastor, right?—but I finally decided that what I have to do is go out and start talking about these things myself, so since then, that's what I've been doing.

MK: I wish you were here on a Sunday. I could take you to my good Latin Mass parish here. I think you would like it.

CML: I was twice baptized to Catholic way back when, but it's like I say, I don't—I was a kid. One of my aunts was a nun, Aunt Sybil, right? I have some fond memories of what it's like to be a real Catholic, but I don't think that that kind of Catholicism is in vogue.

MK: It's certainly not in vogue. When young people are searching for meaning—as you say, you looked for meaning in your life—reminds me of Victor Frankl, right? *Man's Search For Meaning* says, "Search for meaning is man's primary motivator, more than sex, more than anything else." [paraphrase]

CML: And that's the way it should be, but that's not the way it is anymore. They just want the money. They won't even believe that you're intelligent if you don't have a lot of money.

MK: Right. Well, that's what people always ask you, "Why aren't you a billionaire?"

THE INTERVIEW

CML: Why aren't I a billionaire?

MK: That's what people—I've seen people—

CML: Because billionaires hate my guts. See— (*laughs*) I don't go along with the—look, they have to give you the opportunity to make money. You need to have connections. In order to make money, you need to make friends out of people who have a lot of it.

MK: If you had the connections, would you have striven to make money?

CML: Not at the expense of truth. No, I'd have gone after meaning first. Now, I used to think that, *Well, it should be possible in theory to go after both*, then I discovered that wasn't necessarily true. If you go after truth too hard, then you're going to make a bad impression on Mammon, on the people with all the money, and eventually you're going to be cancelled out of any sort of comfortable life.

MK: And isn't—there's also just a time issue, right? I mean, if you dedicate yourself to—I don't know—doing spreadsheets or something, you're probably not going to have a ton of time to pursue truth, or am I wrong about—am I just underestimating—?

CML: You're absolutely right. You know, eventually that's what you become. We are what we do, more or less, so you've got to make up your mind what you want to spend your time doing. I consider it to be better to seek truth, and meaning, and God, than it is to pursue money. Now, who agrees with me these days? Not many people.

MK: I'd like to have it all, but I certainly agree.

CML: Well, I would like to bring mankind back to the point where we care about those things again.

MK: Because, of course, then the question is—if you just focus your life on money, just for money's sake, just to get stuff—you can't take it with you. (*laughs*) Eventually, all that stuff is going to decay.

CML: Well, yes, of course it is. But a lot of these rich people are into something called transhumanism. They don't think that they're going to have to leave, so there's no problem (*smiles*) with not being able to take it with you, because you're not going anywhere. You're going to upload your consciousness to a computer, you see.

MK: I've heard this. It's a very popular idea. A lot of my young friends will tell me, "Michael, we might not even die," as though every generation in history hasn't had the same delusion, but it's all—I always laugh at it. But very wealthy, very powerful, ostensibly intelligent people take this seriously, "We're just going to upload our brain—"

CML: Ostensibly intelligent.

MK: Osten— (*laughs*) That's an important caveat. You don't think we're just going to upload our brains to the cloud or something?

CML: You know, that's what reality already is.

MK: We've already done it.

CML: Self-simulation. We've already done it. We are living in

THE INTERVIEW

the display of a simulation—a Self-simulating Universe—and we going to be uploaded when we're done with this simulat—we're going to be uploaded to the source of all truth, meaning, and power. Then depending on the decision that is made by that entity, we can be redistributed to another universe, a heaven, a hell—

MK: A new creation.

CML: Pardon me?

MK: A new creation. The idea of the resurrection of the body, right?

CML: That is correct.

MK: So before these genius gazillionaires who fancy that they're going to upload their brains to the IBM computer or something, before they meet their particular judgment, before they shuffle off this mortal coil, do you think there's any chance that they're going to figure out the secret and not have to face death?

CML: No.

MK: No way?

CML: It's like I say, Soros is probably the best among them, and he's way—he's far—you know how it is—I mean, I guess the Hindus had a better way of looking at this. In Christianity, there's one goal: salvation. In Hinduism, there are four goals. Okay. You've got *Kama*, *Artha*, *Dharma*, and *Moksha*. And *Kama* is sensual pleasure, and *Artha* is being able to acquire wealth and power. Then you've got *Dharma*, which is righteousness, and then above *Dharma*, you've got *Moksha*, which is salvation. That's actual union with the absolute or with God. The people running the world right now—all of these people that you just mentioned—are stuck in numbers one and two. They haven't made it to *Dharma* and they're never going to make it to *Moksha*. That's why they want to upload their consciousness to a machine. They know that God isn't going to take them back, if they continue doing what they're doing. So they want to displace reality itself by recreating reality in a mechanical form that then they can control.

MK: Do you think there's any relation between the transhumanist movement and the transgender movement, the idea that we're just going to escape our bodies?

CML: Yes, I do. The idea, I think, is that you can throw off all constraint. You can throw off the constraints of reality, including constraints of gender. That's what I think the commonality is, and I think these are—they're anti-teleological, both of them.

MK: I agree.

CML: We do have certain constraints. Reality is full of constraints and we're better off recognizing what they are.

MK: Before I let you go as we sit here in the clouds—in some simulation of the clouds here—before I let you go, people are going to be asking, "So what do I do? What should I do right now?" assuming we're not going to launch the second American Revolution, or anything like that, "What should I do in my own life?" even maybe beyond any political questions.

CML: Search for God. Ask God to establish a personal relationship with you. It's available. You're attached to God by your soul. There's this soul that attaches you to God. You can receive the Will of God into yourself, and to some extent, the power of God into yourself, but you've got to be receptive. If you're not receptive, then you're cutting yourself off from God, and once you do that, then you do not share the identity of reality itself, and you're done. Once your physical body expires, there is nothing that will carry you because you have denied it and rejected it. You follow me?

MK: I do.

CML: That's what people need to do.

MK: I do. I think that's good advice.

CML: I'm glad you agree. That's good for you. (*both laugh*)

MK: It's good. It's sort of like reaching out and grabbing, (*shakes an imaginary listener*) "Do THIS. Search for God," as though to shake the audience.

Chris, this has been a true pleasure. Thank you for coming out. Thank you for making the trek.

CML: Well, it's been my pleasure. I don't travel very often. I've told you the reasons for that, but I'm glad I made this trip, Michael.

MK: Thank you, Chris. (*shake hands*)

REFERENCES

Selected articles and papers

Langan, C. M. (1989) The Resolution of Newcomb's Paradox. *Noesis*, No. 44.

Langan, C. M. (1999) Introduction to the CTMU. *Ubiquity*, Vol. 1, № 1.

Langan, C. M. (2002) *The Cognitive-Theoretic Model of the Universe: A New Kind of Reality Theory*. Princeton, MO: Mega Foundation Press. Originally published in *Progress in Complexity, Information, and Design*, Double Issue, Vols. 1.2-3.

Langan, C. M. (2003) Cheating the Millennium: The Mounting Explanatory Debts of Scientific Naturalism. In W. A. Dembski (Ed.) *Uncommon Dissent: Intellectuals Who Find Darwinism Unconvincing*. Wilmington, DE: ISI Books.

Langan, C. M. (2017) An Introduction to Mathematical Metaphysics. Cosmos and History: *The Journal of Natural and Social Philosophy*, Vol. 13, No. 2, pp. 313-330.

Langan, C. M. (2018a) Metareligion as the Human

Singularity. *Cosmos and History: The Journal of Natural and Social Philosophy*, Vol. 14, No. 1, pp. 321-332.

Langan, C. M. (2018b) The Metaformal System: Completing the Theory of Language. *Cosmos and History: The Journal of Natural and Social Philosophy*, Vol. 14, No. 2, pp. 207-227.

Langan, C. M. (2019) Introduction to Quantum Metamechanics (QMM). *Cosmos and History: The Journal of Natural and Social Philosophy*, Vol. 15, No. 1, pp. 265-300.

Langan, C. M. (2020) The Reality Self-Simulation Principle: Reality is a Self-Simulation. *Cosmos and History: The Journal of Natural and Social Philosophy*, Vol. 16, No. 1, pp. 466-486.

Other authors

Descartes, R. (1996) *Meditations on First Philosophy with Selections from the Objections and Replies*. Edited by J. Cottingham. Cambridge: Cambridge University Press.

Einstein A. (1920) *Relativity: The Special and the General Theory: A Popular Exposition*. London: Methuen & Co., Ltd.

Einstein A. (1954) *Ideas and Opinions* New York: Crown Publishers

Frankl, V. A. (1959) *Man's Search for Meaning: An Introduction to Logotherapy*. Translated by Ilse Lasch. Boston, MA: Beacon Press.

Gödel, K. (1962) *On Formally Undecidable Propositions of Principia Mathematica and Related Systems*. Translated by B. Meltzer. New York: Basic Books.

REFERENCES

Russell, B. (1959) *The Problems of Philosophy*. New York: Oxford University Press.

Russell, B. (1961) *History of Western Philosophy and its Connection with Political and Social Circumstances from the Earliest Times to the Present Day*. London: Allen & Unwin Ltd.

Internet sources

At the time this book went to press, the below links worked.

Aristotle (350 B.C.E) The Internet Classics Archive, https://classics.mit.edu/Browse/browse-Aristotle.html

Milton J. (1674) *Paradise Lost*. Book One. Poetry Foundation, https://www.poetryfoundation.org/poems/45718/paradise-lost-book-1-1674-version

Langan, C. M. (2022) High Strangeness at the Daily Wire. Chris Langan's Ultimate Reality, https://chrislangan.substack.com/p/high-strangeness-at-the-daily-wire

Plato (1946) *The Republic*. [written 360 B.C.E] The Internet Classics Archive. Translated by Benjamin Jowett, https://classics.mit.edu/Plato/republic.html

Plotinus (1952) *The Six Enneads*. [written 250 A.C.E.] The Internet Classics Archive. Translated by Stephen Mackenna and B. S. Page, https://classics.mit.edu/Plotinus/enneads.html

Thomas Aquinas (2020) *Summa Theologiae*. [written between 1265 and 1273] Aquinas Institute, Inc., https://aquinas.cc/la/en/~ST.I

Printed in Great Britain
by Amazon